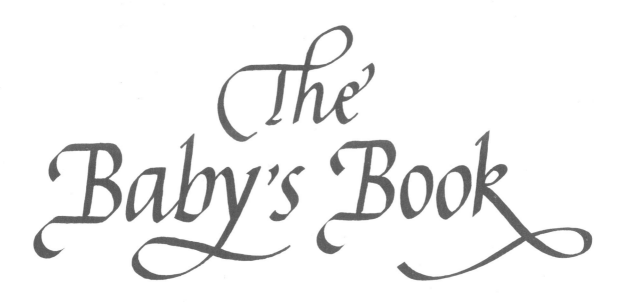

The Baby's Book

BY
MARCIA O. LEVIN

HUGH LAUTER LEVIN ASSOCIATES, INC., NEW YORK

DISTRIBUTED BY
THE SCRIBNER BOOK COMPANIES

ILLUSTRATIONS

Mary Cassatt
BABY CHARLES LOOKING OVER HIS MOTHER'S
SHOULDER (No. 3)
c. 1900
oil on canvas
27⅛ × 20⅜"
Collection: The Brooklyn Museum; Carl H. DeSilver Fund

Pablo Picasso
MOTHER AND CHILD
1921
oil on canvas
56½ × 64"
The Art Institute of Chicago
© S.P.A.D.E.M., Paris/V.A.G.A., New York 1984

Berthe-Marie-Pauline Morisot
THE CRADLE
1873
oil on canvas
21½ × 18"
The Louvre, Paris
Courtesy: Service de Documentation Photographique de la
Réunion des Musées Nationaux, Paris

Mary Cassatt
MATERNAL CARESS
1891
color print with drypoint, soft-ground, and aquatint
14⅜ × 10½"
National Gallery of Art, Washington, D.C.; Gift of Miss
Elisabeth Achelis 1942

Mary Cassatt
BABY REACHING FOR AN APPLE
1893
oil on canvas
39½ × 25¾"
Virginia Museum of Fine Arts, Richmond; Gift of Anonymous
Donor 1975

Milton Avery
MOTHER AND CHILD
1944
oil on canvas
40 × 30"
Private Collection, Courtesy: Andrew Crispo Gallery, Inc., New
York

Grandma Moses
ROCKABYE
1957
oil on masonite
11⅞ × 16"
Private Collection
Copyright © 1973, Grandma Moses Properties Co., New York.

Mary Cassatt
LITTLE ANN SUCKING HER FINGER, EMBRACED BY HER
MOTHER
1897
pastel on beige paper
21¾ × 17"
Collection: Jeu de Paume Museum, Paris
Courtesy: Service de Documentation Photographique de la Réunion
des Musées Nationaux, Paris

Mary Cassatt
BABY'S FIRST CARESS
1891
pastel on paper
30 × 24"
New Britain Museum of American Art, Connecticut; Harriett
Russell Stanley Fund

Auguste Renoir
GABRIELLE ET JEAN
oil on canvas
Grenoble Museum
Courtesy: Art Resource, New York

Mary Cassatt
BABY IN DARK BLUE SUIT
1889
oil on canvas
29 × 23½"
Cincinnati Art Museum; Gift of John J. Emery Endowment

Edmund Charles Tarbell
MOTHER AND CHILD IN A BOAT
1892
oil on canvas
30 × 35"
Museum of Fine Arts, Boston; Bequest of David B. Kimball
in memory of his wife, Clara Bertram Kimball.

Maurice Prendergast
LARGE BOSTON PUBLIC GARDEN SKETCHBOOK, page 29
Woman pushing a perambulator and talking to a little girl.
c. 1895–97
watercolor on paper
14¼ × 11¼"
The Metropolitan Museum of Art; Robert Lehman Collection, 1975.

Pablo Picasso
MOTHER AND CHILD
Dinard, Summer 1922
oil on canvas
39½ × 31½"
The Baltimore Museum of Art; The Cone Collection, formed
by Dr. Claribel Cone and Miss Etta Cone of Baltimore, Maryland.
© S.P.A.D.E.M., Paris/V.A.G.A., New York 1984

Calligraphy by *Calligraphy Studios*
NEW YORK

Printed in Japan

ISBN 0-88363-084-2

Page 46

One Foot, Other Foot
© 1948 by Richard Rodgers and Oscar Hammerstein II. Williamson
Music Co., owner of publication and allied rights throughout the
Western Hemisphere and Japan. International Copyright Secured. All
rights reserved. Used by permission.

Page 51

Happy Talk
© 1949 by Richard Rodgers and Oscar Hammerstein II. Williamson
Music Co., owner of publication and allied rights throughout the
Western Hemisphere and Japan. International Copyright Secured. All
rights reserved. Used by permission.

Page 54

My Favorite Things
© 1959 by Richard Rodgers and Oscar Hammerstein II. Williamson
Music Co., owner of publication and allied rights throughout the
Western Hemisphere and Japan. International Copyright Secured. All
rights reserved. Used by permission.

Dedication

This book tells what happened
from the day you were born until
you were one year old.

Some day you will be able to
read about these things by yourself.

And in a few years, years that
will pass very slowly for you, but very
quickly for us, perhaps you will show
this book to a child of your own.

BABY CHARLES LOOKING OVER HIS MOTHER'S SHOULDER—Mary Cassatt

This book belongs to

Anna Kathryn David

Monday's child is fair of face
Tuesday's child is full of grace
Wednesday's child is full of woe
Thursday's child has far to go
Friday's child is loving and giving
Saturday's child works hard for a living
But the child who is born on the Sabbath day
Is bonny and blithe, and good and gay.

When

THURSDAY	11:23 A	MAY	10	1969
Day of the week	Hour	Month	Day	Year

Where

New York Hospital
Place

535 E 68TH St, NY, NY
Address

Who Helped To Deliver You

Name _DR. TERRI EDERSHEIM_

Address _____

Signature _____

Name _____

Address _____

Signature _____

Name _____

Address _____

Signature _____

Name _____

Address _____

Signature _____

Your Name

First _____

Middle _____

Last _____

Your name was chosen by

_____

You were given your name because

_____

Your name means

_____

Your Handprint   *Your Footprint*

9

MOTHER AND CHILD—Pablo Picasso

Birth Information

Color of hair _____ Blonde _____

Color of eyes _____ blue _____

Weight _____ 7 pounds 5 oz. _____

Length _____ 16¾ inches _____

Identifying marks _____

Your First Picture

Paste Photo Here

Date _____

Taken at _____

The First Time We Saw You

Mother said

_____

_____

_____

_____

Father said

_____

_____

_____

_____

THE CRADLE—Berthe-Marie-Pauline Morisot

Paste
Birth Certificate
Here

Paste
Birth Announcement
Here

Your Horoscope

The day you were born

Paste
Horoscope
Here

Printed in _____

Your zodiac sign _____

Your birthstone _____

16

MOTHER AND CHILD—Milton Avery

Headlines in the News

The day you were born

World events

_____

_____

_____

Local events

_____

_____

_____

Weather that day

_____

_____

What the World Was Like

President of the United States

Vice-President of the United States

Popular Songs

Most popular films and plays

Most popular actors and actresses

Best-selling books

Latest fad

What women were wearing

What men were wearing

How people traveled

Zana Blackwell

Name of Grandmother's Mother (your great-grandma)	Name of Grandmother's Father (your great-grandpa)	Name of Grandfather's Mother (your great-grandma)	Name of Grandfather's Father (your great-grandpa)
June 3, 1888			
Birth Date	Birth Date	Birth Date	Birth Date
Birth Place	Birth Place	Birth Place	Birth Place

Kathryn Morgan Weiss

Name of Mother's Mother
(your grandmother)

James Augustus Weiss

Name of Mother's Father
(your grandfather)

July 22,

Birth Date

Copperhill, Tennessee

Birth Date

Ducktown Tn

Birth Place

Birth Place

Cecilia Weiss David

Mother's Full Name

April 5, 1953

Birth Date

Sacramento, Cal

Birth Place

BABY REACHING FOR AN APPLE—Mary Cassatt

Father's Family Tree

Name of
Grandmother's Mother
(your great-grandma)

Name of
Grandmother's Father
(your great-grandpa)

Name of
Grandfather's Mother
(your great-grandma)

Name of
Grandfather's Father
(your great-grandpa)

Birth Date

Birth Date

Birth Date

Birth Date

Birth Place

Birth Place

Birth Place

Birth Place

Name of Father's Mother
(your grandmother)

Name of Father's Father
(your grandfather)

Birth Date

Birth Date

Birth Place

Birth Place

Father's Full Name

Birth Date

Birth Place

Other Relatives

Name	How Related	Birth Date

How many miles to Baby-land?
Anyone can tell
Up one flight,
To your right;
Please to ring the bell.

Who is the Queen of Baby-land?
Mother kind and sweet;
And her love,
Born above,
Guides the little feet.

George Cooper

Gift	From
Sterling Silver Cup	Kathy, Andrea & Dana
Quilt - Hand made	Grandma Betty
Cookie Monster	Chris
Big Bird	Michael

MATERNAL CARESS—*Mary Cassatt*

Visitors

and what they said about you

_____

_____

_____

_____

_____

_____

_____

_____

_____

_____

Visitors

and what they said about you

Who Took Care of You

At the beginning

    Name _MICHAEL F. DAVID_

    Relationship _FATHER_

    Your reaction _____

Who helped

    Name _KATHY WEISS_

    Relationship _AUNT_

    Your reaction _____

As you got bigger

    Name _BETTY & WILFRED DAVID_

    Relationship _GRANDPARENTS_

    Name _____

    Relationship _____

    Name _____

    Relationship _____

ROCKABYE—*Grandma Moses*

Street _24 Bynon Road_

City _Maplewood_

State _New Jersey_

When we moved there

March 17, 1964

What you liked best about this place

Paste Photo Here

A Typical Day

6 A.M. _____   6 P.M. _____

7 A.M. _____   7 P.M. _____

8 A.M. _____   8 P.M. _____

9 A.M. _____   9 P.M. _____

10 A.M. _____   10 P.M. _____

11 A.M. _____   11 P.M. _____

12 Noon _____   12 Midnight _____

1 P.M. _____   1 A.M. _____

2 P.M. _____   2 A.M. _____

3 P.M. _____   3 A.M. _____

4 P.M. _____   4 A.M. _____

5 P.M. _____   5 A.M. _____

Medical Information

Doctor's Name _____

Address _____

Telephone _____

Dates of Visits	What the Doctor Said

6·26·69

Accidents and Illnesses

When I was sick and lay a-bed,
I had two pillows at my head,
And all my toys about me lay
To keep me happy all the day.

Robert Louis Stevenson

Date   What Happened   Treatment

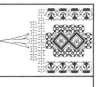

Medical Record

Inoculations:	Dates	Dates of Boosters
DPT { Diptheria		
Whooping Cough		
Tetanus		
Polio		
Measles		
Rubella		
Rubeola		
Other		

Tests:	Dates	Results
Tuberculin		
Others		
Blood type	8/6/09	A- POSITIVE
Allergies		

Dental Record

Dental Chart

Central Incisor
at _____ months

Central Incisor
at _____ months

Lateral Incisor
at _____ months

Lateral Incisor
at _____ months

Cuspid
at _____ months

Cuspid
at _____ months

First Molar
at _____ months

First Molar
at _____ months

Upper

First Molar
at _____ months

Lower

First Molar
at _____ months

Cuspid
at _____ months

Cuspid
at _____ months

Lateral Incisor
at _____ months

Lateral Incisor
at _____ months

Central Incisor
at _____ months

Central Incisor
at _____ months

Teething Problems _____

_____

_____

LITTLE ANN SUCKING HER FINGER, EMBRACED BY HER MOTHER—Mary Cassatt

Bye, baby bunting
Daddy's gone a-hunting.
To get a little rabbit skin
To wrap the baby bunting in.

What	When
Lifted your head	from birth
Grasped someone's finger	birth
Looked at things overhead	6/4
Rolled to one side	
Recognized Mother or Dad	

Paste Photo Here

Brow brinkie,
Eye winkie,
Mouth merry,
Cheek Cherry,
Chin-chopper, chin-chopper,
Chin-chopper chin.

(Say this rhyme as you
point to baby's features)

What   When

Held your head steady   _____

Rolled onto your tummy   _____

Sat, propped up   _____

Recognized people who
took care of you   _____

Paste Photo Here

Ride a cock horse
To Banbury Cross,
To see a fine lady
Ride on a white horse.

What   When

Liked to bounce on
   someone's knee   _____

Reached for a toy   _____

Liked to bite   _____

Banged a toy on
   a table top   _____

Paste Photo Here

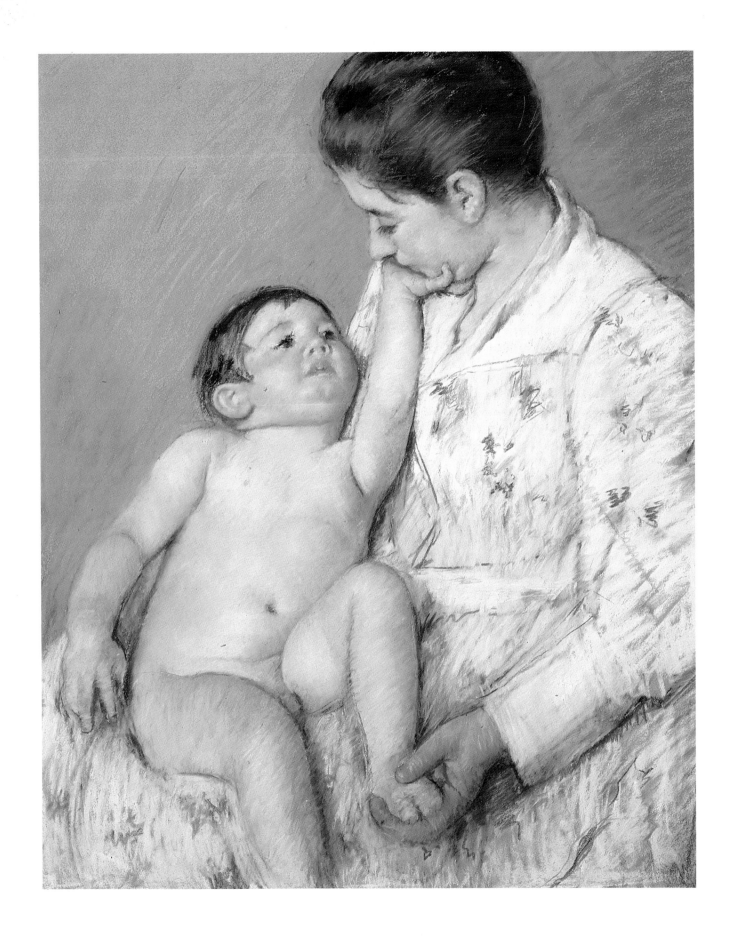

BABY'S FIRST CARESS—Mary Cassatt

"Where's the baby?"   "Here (s)he is!"

What   When

    Played "Where's the baby?"
      (or "Peek-a-boo!")   _____

    Recognized familiar faces   _____

    Sat up by yourself   _____

    Got up on your hands and knees _____

    Hit two blocks together   _____

Paste Photo Here

42

Pat-a-cake, pat-a-cake, baker's man,
Bake me a cake as fast as you can;
Pat it and prick it, and mark it with a B,
And put it in the oven for Baby and me.

What   When

 Played pat-a-cake   _____

 Began to crawl   _____

 Pulled yourself up with support _____

 Piled one block on top of another _____

 Threw things out of your
   highchair or bed   _____

Paste Photo Here

Hickory dickory dock;
The mouse ran up the clock.
The clock struck one;
The mouse ran down,
Hickory dickory dock.

What   When

   Enjoyed rhymes

   Walked with one hand held   _____

   Gave someone a toy when asked   _____

   Put beads into a box   _____

   Held out an arm when being dressed   _____

Paste Photo Here

GABRIELLE ET JEAN—*Auguste Renoir*

Now you can go wherever you want
Wherever you want to go
One foot out and the other foot out
That's all you need to know.

Oscar Hammerstein
"Allegro"

Took your first step alone _____
When

Paste Photo Here

The Way You Grew

How big is the baby? Soooo big!

Age	Height	Weight
1 month		9 lbs.
2 months		
3 months		
4 months		
5 months		
6 months		
7 months		
8 months		
9 months		
10 months		
11 months		

At one year, you weighed _____

Your height was _____

47

The Way You Slept

Sleep, baby, sleep;
Thy father tends the sheep.
Thy mother tends the dreamland tree,
And from it fall sweet dreams for thee;
Sleep, baby, sleep.

When

You slept through one of the night feedings _____

You slept through the night _____

Your morning nap changed _____

Your favorite way to sleep was _____

_____

Your bedtime toys were _____

_____

Other comments _____

_____

_____

BABY IN DARK BLUE SUIT—Mary Cassatt

A child should always say what's true.
And speak when he is spoken to,
And behave mannerly at table :
At least so far as he is able.

Robert Louis Stevenson

What   When

You began to chew food   _____
You ate from a spoon and fork _____
You drank from a cup   _____
You held your own spoon   _____
You held your own cup   _____
You drank by yourself   _____
You fed yourself   _____
Your first "real" food was _____

_____

The foods you liked best were _____

_____

The foods you liked least were _____

_____

Comments _____

_____

Happy talk, keep talking happy talk.
Talk about things you like to do.
You've got to have a dream
If you don't have a dream
How're you going to make a dream come true?

Oscar Hammerstein
"South Pacific"

What you did	When
Made cooing sounds	_____
Laughed	_____
Noticed voices	_____
Said mmmmmmm	_____
Made other sounds	_____
Said Da-da	_____

When you were one year old,
 you could say _____

_____

_____

The Places You Visited

You, friendly Earth, how far do you go,
With wheat fields that nod and rivers that flow,
With cities, and gardens, and cliffs, and isles,
And people upon you for thousands of miles?

Matthew Browne

Your first trip outdoors was *foodshopping @ Pathmark*

_____

The ride you took most often was _____

_____

You liked to ride in _____

_____

Your favorite place to visit was _____

_____

_____

Your longest trip was _____

_____

_____

MOTHER AND CHILD IN A BOAT—Edmund Charles Tarbell

Your Favorite Things

Raindrops on roses and whiskers on kittens,
Bright copper kettles and warm woolen mittens,
Brown paper packages tied up with string
These are a few of my favorite things.

Oscar Hammerstein
"The Sound of Music"

Your favorite toys _____

_____

Your favorite games _____

_____

Your favorite rhymes _____

_____

Your favorite books _____

Your favorite animals _____

Your favorite people _____

_____

Your First Birthday

The weather that day _____

_____

Where you were _____

_____

What you wore _____

_____

Who was there _____

_____

_____

_____

What you did _____

_____

_____

How you acted _____

_____

_____

Your gifts _____

_____

_____

_____

_____

Your Schedule at One Year

A Typical Day

Morning

_____

_____

_____

_____

_____

Afternoon

_____

_____

_____

_____

_____

Evening

_____

_____

_____

_____

_____

Night

_____

_____

_____

_____

_____

WOMAN PUSHING A PERAMBULATOR AND TALKING TO A LITTLE GIRL—Maurice Prendergast

We'll Always Remember

Your reaction to _____

_____

What you did when _____

_____

What you said when _____

_____

The funniest thing that happened
to you was _____

_____

_____

The cutest thing you did was _____

_____

_____

_____

_____

We want you to remember that:

Every flutter of the wing,
Every note of song we sing,
Every murmur, every tone,
Is of love, and love alone.

Henry Wadsworth Longfellow

We will always love you as
much as we have loved you
during your first wonderful year.

Afterthoughts

Milestones, comments and memorable events
as you grew :

MOTHER AND CHILD—*Pablo Picasso*

Afterthoughts

Milestones, comments and memorable events
as you grew:

Afterthoughts

Milestones, comments and memorable events
as you grew:

_____

_____

_____

_____

_____

_____

_____

_____

_____

_____

Afterthoughts

Milestones, comments and memorable events
as you grew:

_____

_____

_____

_____

_____

_____

_____

_____

_____

_____